TO: _____

WITH LOVE: _____

memorythiefbook.com
facebook.com/thememorythief

Credits
Author, Illustrator, Designer: Kyle Herges
ISBN-13: 978-0-692-48533-0

This book is dedicated to all those diagnosed with Alzheimer's disease and anyone caring for those with Alzheimer's disease. My grandpa was diagnosed with Alzheimer's and fought the memory thief for ten years before ultimately losing his battle. My mom was diagnosed with early onset Alzheimer's disease at the age of 58 and continues to fight.

Each page has a keyword, or words, marked in purple. The graphic is directly related to that keyword or words. The goal is to engage children of all ages to ask questions using words they understand.

A portion of each sale will go to support finding a cure for Alzheimer's disease. Statistics provided by alz.org. Find more information or make a donation at **alz.org.**

My words are **scrambled** and things are changing.

I'm sure you've noticed I'm not as **engaging**.

My mind's not as **sharp** as it used to be.

This memory **thief** has its firm grip on me.

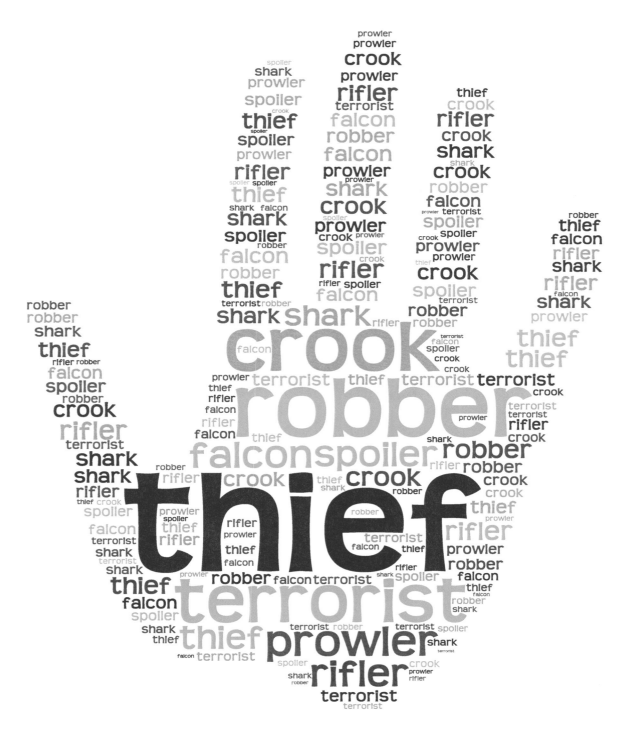

I'll begin to forget **memories**, **stories** and **places**.

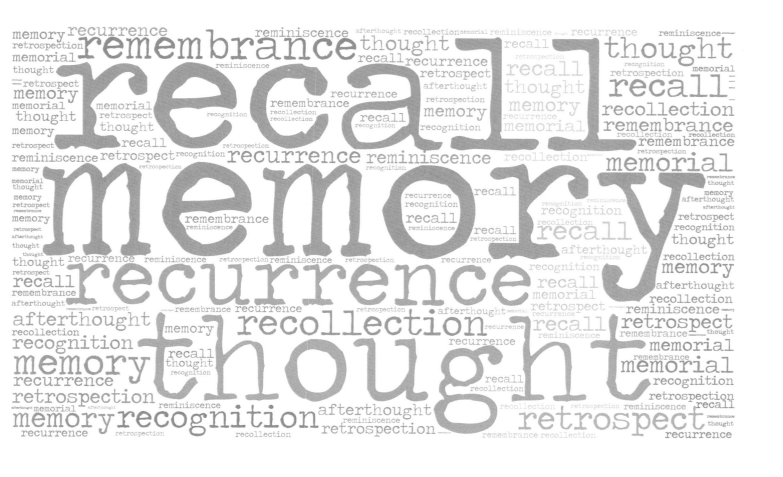

I'll even start to **forget** some of your faces.

I may stop calling you each by **name**.

But know that I'll still **love you**
just the same.

Don't be **scared**, **angry** or **upset**.

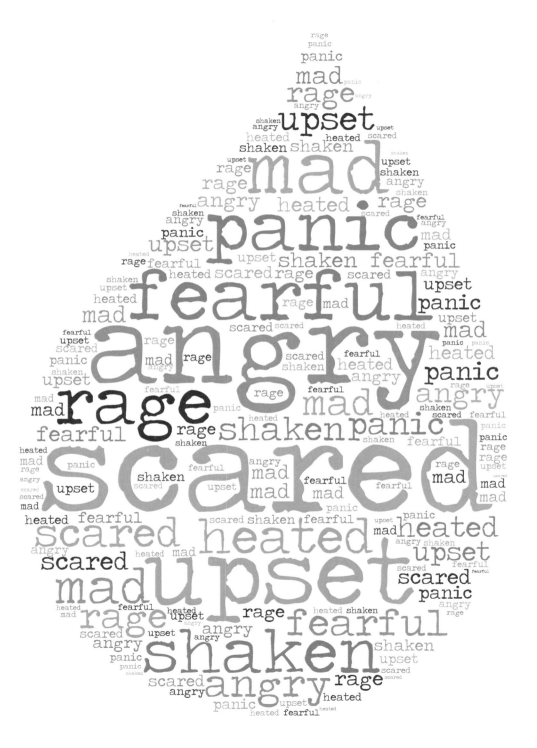

Let's just **cherish** the time
we have left.

My **heart** keeps the real memories
that I shall save.

Because it's you, my dear,
who keeps me so **brave**.

Just hug, **smile**, love.
And I will too.

God has a plan.
Trust is all we can do.

outline
outline
idea
heaven
plan
idea design
God
scheme
method design
trust outline God
trust
idea
God arrangement
trust
plan
arrangement
God
heaven
method
design
idea
heaven
scheme
design
idea
God
God
plan
God
heaven heaven
God
arrangement
design
trust
idea
idea
arrangement
trust
scheme
method
outline
design
heaven
scheme
design
plan
trust plan method
scheme
God
heaven trust heaven
scheme
method
trust
scheme outline
method
arrangement
design plan
outline
plan method

So when it's time for my **spirit** to take over,

I'll be in heaven – an **angel** on your shoulder.

I Love You.

Quick Facts

Facts courtesy of http://www.alz.org.

Alzheimer's disease is the 6th leading cause of death in the United States and **KILLS MORE PEOPLE THAN BREAST CANCER AND PROSTATE CANCER COMBINED.**

ALMOST TWO THIRDS of Americans with Alzheimer's disease are women.

EVERY

67

SECONDS someone in the United States develops the disease.

In thirteen years, Alzheimer's **DEATHS INCREASED BY**

71%

This year, Alzheimer's and other dementias will cost the nation **$228 BILLION.**

By 2050, these costs could rise as high as **$1.1 TRILLION.**

Of America's top 10 causes of death, Alzheimer's disease is the only one that **CANNOT BE PREVENTED, CURED OR SLOWED.**

REVIEW →

 NO PREVENTION

 NO CURE

 NO SLOWING

250,000

CHILDREN & YOUNG ADULTS

between ages 8 and 18 provide help to someone with Alzheimer's disease or another dementia.

Made in the USA
Lexington, KY
18 September 2017